PREPARED LEADERSHIP;
Amazing Crisis Management and Emergency Planning.

Lillian R. Murray

All rights reserved. No part of this publication may be reproduced, distributed, or transmitted in any form or by any means, including photocopying, recording, or other electronic or mechanical methods, without the prior written permission of the publisher, except in the case of brief quotations embodied in critical reviews and certain other noncommercial uses permitted by copyright law.

Copyright ©Lillian R. Murray,2022.

Table of Content

Chapter 1 –CRISIS MANAGEMENT

— What Crisis Management Truly Is.

Chapter 2—Phases of Crisis Management

1. pre-crisis phase

2. crisis response,

Chapter 3— 3. post-crisis.

Chapter 4—CRISIS MANAGEMENT PLAN

—Pre– draft Messages

Chapter5—BUILDING A CRISIS MANAGEMENT TEAM.

1. Spoke person

2. Communication Channel

3. Post- Crisis and Resolution

4. Reputation Repair and Behavioral Intention

Chapter 6—BEST PRACTICES FOR ALL THE PHASES OF CRISIS

Chapter 7— 7 STEPS TO CRISIS MANAG—MANAGEMENT

Chapter 8— LESSONS LEARNED IN CRISIS MANAGEMENT.

1. Need for Crisis Management

2. Essential features of Crisis Managements

3. Points to keep in mind during crisis

INTRODUCTION

Crisis Management is a basic hierarchical capability. Disappointment can bring about serious mischief to partners, misfortunes for an association, or end its actual presence. Advertising specialists are a basic piece of emergency supervisory crews. So a bunch of best practices and illustrations gathered from our insight into emergency the board would be an exceptionally helpful asset for those in advertising. Volumes have been expounded on emergency the board by the two specialists and scientists from various disciplines making it a test to combine emergency the executives and advertising's place in that information base. The best spot to begin this work is by characterizing basic ideas.

Chapter 1

CRISIS MANAGEMENT
What Crisis Management Truely Is;

Crisis management is the utilization of methodologies intended to assist an association with managing an unexpected and huge adverse occasion.

An emergency can happen because of an unusual occasion or an unforeseeable outcome of some occasion that had been considered as a possible gamble. Regardless, emergencies perpetually expect that choices be made rapidly to restrict harm to the association.

The idea of the potential harm shifts in view of the idea of the emergency. Much of the time however, an emergency can influence wellbeing or security, the association's funds, the association's standing, or a mix of these. A staggering fire could be an emergency that places the association's funds in danger. Be that as it may, in the event that the fire happens during business hours, the fire could likewise risk wellbeing and security since representatives might end up in danger.

There are a lot of definitions for an emergency. For this passage, the definition reflects central issues found in the different conversations of what is an emergency. An emergency is characterized here as a huge danger to tasks that can have unfortunate results in the event that not dealt with as expected. In emergency the executives, the danger is the potential harm an emergency can cause for an association, its partners, and an industry. An emergency can make three related dangers: (1) public wellbeing, (2) monetary misfortune, and (3) notoriety misfortune. A few emergencies, for example, modern mishaps and item hurt, can bring about wounds and even loss of lives. Emergencies can make monetary misfortune by disturbing tasks, making a deficiency of piece of the pie/buy expectations, or producing claims connected with the emergency. As verified in The Corporate Correspondences Book of scriptures, all emergencies take steps to discolor an association's standing.

An emergency ponders inadequately an association and will harm a standing somewhat. Obviously these three dangers are interrelated. Wounds or passings will result in monetary and notoriety misfortune while notorieties monetarily affect organizations.Effective emergency the executives handles the dangers consecutively. The essential worry in an emergency must be public wellbeing. An inability to address public wellbeing heightens the harm from an emergency.

Notoriety and monetary worries are viewed as after open security has been helped. Eventually, emergency the board is intended to safeguard an association and its partners from dangers or potentially decrease the effect felt by threats. Crisis the executives is an interaction intended to forestall or reduce the harm an emergency can cause for an association and its partners. As a cycle, emergency the board isn't only a certain something. Crisis management can be divided into three phases:

(1) pre-crisis,
(2) crisis response, and
(3) post-crisis.

The pre-crisis phase isworried about anticipation and readiness. The emergency reaction stage is when the board should really answer an emergency. The post-emergency stage searches for ways of bettering plan for the following emergency and satisfies responsibilities made during the emergency stage including follow-up data. The tri-part perspective on emergency the board fills in as the getting sorted out system for this section.

Chapter 2

PRE-CRISIS PHASE

worried about counteraction and arrangement. The emergency reaction stage is when the executives should really answer an emergency. The post-emergency stage searches for ways of bettering plan for the following emergency and satisfies responsibilities made during the emergency stage including follow-up data. The tri-part perspective on emergency the executives fills in as the getting sorted out structure for this passage.

CRISIS RESPONSE

The emergency reaction is what the executives does and says after the emergency hits. Advertising assumes a basic part in the emergency reaction by assisting with fostering the messages that are shipped off different publics. A lot of examination has inspected the emergency reaction. That examination has been separated into two areas: (1) the initial crisis response and (2) reputation repair and behavioral intentions .

INITIAL RESPONSE

Expert experience and scholarly exploration have consolidated to make a reasonable arrangement of rules for how to answer once an emergency hits. The underlying emergency reaction rules center around three focuses: (1) be speedy, (2) be exact, and (3) be consistent. Be fast appears to be fairly straightforward, give a reaction in the primary hour after the emergency happens. That comes down on emergency directors to have a message prepared in a brief timeframe. Once more, we can see the value in the worth of planning and formats. The reasoning behind being speedy is the requirement for the association to recount its side of the story. Truly, the association's side of the story are the central issues the executives needs to pass about the emergency on to its partners. At the point when an emergency happens, individuals need to realize what occurred. Emergency specialists frequently discuss a data vacuum being made by an emergency.

The news media will lead the charge to fill the data vacuum and be a vital wellspring of starting emergency data. On the off chance that the association having the emergency doesn't address the news media, others will be glad to converse with the media. These individuals might have wrong data or may attempt to involve the emergency as a chance to go after the association. Thus, emergency supervisors should have a fast reaction. An early reaction might not have a lot "new" data but rather the association positions itself as a source and presents its side of the story.

A fast reaction is dynamic and shows an association is in charge. Quiet is excessively latent. It allows others to control the story and recommends the association presently can't seem to oversee what is going on. Early reaction permits an association to create more prominent validity than a sluggish reaction. Emergency readiness will make it simpler for emergency chiefs to answer quickly.Obviously precision is significant whenever an association speaks with publics. Individuals need precise data about what occurred and what that occasion could mean for them. Due to the time tension in an emergency, there is a gamble of erroneous data. Assuming that slip-ups are made, they should be amended. In any case, errors make an association look conflicting. Erroneous proclamations should be rectified causing an association to seem, by all accounts, to be inept.

The way of thinking of talking with one voice in an emergency is a method for keeping up with accuracy.Speaking with one voice doesn't mean just a single individual represents the association as long as necessary. It is truly difficult to anticipate that one individual should represent an association assuming an emergency goes on for more than a day. Watch news inclusion of an emergency and you undoubtedly will see various individuals talk. The news media need to pose inquiries of specialists so they might have to converse with an individual in tasks or one from security.

It stresses that the advertising division plays even more a help job as opposed to being "the" emergency spokespersons. The emergency group necessities to share data with the goal that various individuals can in any case pass on a predictable message. The spokespersons ought to be advised on similar data and the central issues the association is attempting to pass on in the messages. The advertising office ought to be instrumental in setting up the spokespersons. In a perfect world, potential spokespersons are prepared and practice media relations abilities preceding any emergency. The concentration during an emergency then ought to be on the critical data to be conveyed as opposed to how to deal with the media. Yet again planning helps by ensuring the different spokespersons have the appropriate media relations preparing and skills.Quickness and exactness assume a significant part in open security.

At the point when public security is a worry, individuals need to understand how they should safeguard themselves. This data as training data. Training data should be fast and precise to be helpful. For example, individuals should be aware quickly not to eat tainted food sources or to shield set up during a synthetic delivery. A sluggish or mistaken reaction can build the gamble of wounds and conceivably passings. Speedy activities can likewise set aside cash by forestalling further harm and safeguarding notorieties by showing that the association is in charge.

Notwithstanding, speed is negligible in the event that the data is off-base. Wrong data can increment instead of reduction the danger to public safety.The news media are attracted to emergencies and are a valuable method for arriving at a wide exhibit of publics rapidly. So it is legitimate that emergency reaction research has committed impressive thoughtfulness regarding media relations. Media relations permits emergency directors to arrive at many partners quick. Quick and far reaching is ideal for public security — receive the message out rapidly and to however many individuals as could reasonably be expected. Obviously there is squander as non-targets get the message however speed and reach are more significant at the underlying phase of the emergency.

Be that as it may, the news media isn't the main channel emergency directors can and ought to use to arrive at stakeholders.Web destinations, Intranet locales, and mass notice frameworks add to the news media inclusion and assist with giving a fast reaction. Emergency supervisors can supply more noteworthy measures of their own data on a site. Not all objectives will utilize the site yet enough do to legitimize the consideration of web-base correspondence in an emergency reaction.

Broad examination of emergency sites over a long term period found a sluggish movement in associations using sites and the intelligent idea of the web during an emergency. Mass warning frameworks convey short messages to explicit people through a blend of telephone, message informing, voice messages, and email. The frameworks likewise permit individuals to send reactions. In associations with viable Intranet frameworks, the Intranet is a valuable vehicle for arriving at workers too. In the event that an association coordinates its Intranet with providers and clients, these partners can be reached too. As the emergency the executives exertion advances, the channels can be more selective. More as of late, emergency specialists have prescribed a third part to an underlying emergency reaction, emergency chiefs ought to communicate concern/compassion toward any casualties of the emergency. Casualties are individuals that are harmed or burdened here and there by the emergency. Casualties could have lost cash, become not well, needed to clear, or endured property harm.

Articulations of concern help to diminish reputational harm and to decrease monetary misfortunes. Exploratory investigations discovered that associations caused experience less reputational harm when an outflow of concern is offered stanzas a reaction without a declaration of concern. Lawful cases and found early articulations of concern help to diminish the number and measure of cases made against an association for the emergency. Nonetheless, there are cutoff points to articulations of concern.

Legal counselors might attempt to involve articulations of worry as confirmations of culpability. Various states have regulations that safeguard articulations of worry from being utilized against an association. Another worry is that as more emergency administrators express concern, the outflows of concern might lose their impact of individuals. articulations of concern will appear to be excessively standard. All things considered, an inability to give a normal reaction could hurt an association. Consequently, articulations of concern might be normal and give little advantage when utilized however can cause harm when not utilized.. representatives need to realize what occurred, what they ought to do, and what the emergency will mean for them. The previous conversations of mass notice frameworks and the Intranet are instances of how to arrive at workers with data. Also, research that propose all around informed representatives give an extra channel of correspondence for coming to other stakeholders.

When the emergency brings about serious wounds or passings, emergency the board should incorporate pressure and injury directing for workers and different casualties. One representation is the injury groups dispatched via carriers following a plane accident. Note that emergency chiefs should consider what the emergency stress could mean for the workers, casualties, and their families. Associations should give the vital assets to assist these gatherings cope.We with canning take a particular arrangement of both structure and content illustrations from the composition on the underlying emergency reaction.

Table 4 gives a synopsis of the Underlying Emergency Reaction Best Practices. Structure alludes to the fundamental design of the reaction. The underlying emergency reaction ought to be conveyed in the primary hour after an emergency and be reviewed for precision. Content alludes to what is shrouded in the underlying emergency reaction. The underlying message should give any data expected to help public wellbeing, give fundamental data about what has occurred, and offer concern in the event that there are casualties. What's more, emergency directors should attempt to have a reliable message between spokespersons.

Chapter 3

POST-CRISIS PHASE

In the post-crisis phase, the organization is returning to business as usual. The crisis is no longer the focal point of management's attention but still requires some attention. As noted earlier, reputation repair may be continued or initiated during this phase. There is important follow-up communication that is required. First, crisis managers often promise to provide additional information during the crisis phase.

The crisis managers must deliver on those informational promises or risk losing the trust of publics wanting the information. Second, the organization needs to release updates on the recovery process, corrective actions, and/or investigations of the crisis.

The amount of follow-up communication required depends on the amount of information promised during the crisis and the length of time it takes to complete the recovery process. If you promised a reporter a damage estimate, for example, be sure to deliver that estimate when it is ready.

West Pharmaceuticals provided recovery updates for over a year because that is how long it took to build a new facility to replace the one destroyed in an explosion. Intranets are an excellent way to keep employees updated, if the employees have ways to access the site. mass notification systems can be used as well to deliver update messages to employees and other publics via phones, text messages, voice messages, and e-mail. Personal e-mails and phone calls can be used too.Crisis managers agree that a crisis should be a learning experience. The crisis management effort needs to be evaluated to see what is working and what needs improvement.

The same holds true for exercises. every crisis management exercise be carefully dissected as a learning experience. The organization should seek ways to improve prevention, preparation, and/or the response. As most books on crisis management note, those lessons are then integrated into the pre-crisis and crisis response phases. That is how management learns and improves its crisis management process. Table 8 lists the Post-Crisis Phase Best Practices.

.

Chapter 4

CRISIS MANAGEMENT PLAN
A crisis management plan (CMP) is a reference device, not a diagram. A CMP gives arrangements of key contact data, tokens of what ordinarily ought to be finished in an emergency, and structures to be utilized to record the emergency reaction. A CMP is definitely not a bit by bit manual for how to deal with an emergency. noticed how a CMP saves time during an emergency by pre-doling out certain undertakings, pre-gathering some data, and filling in as a kind of perspective source. Pre-relegating undertakings assumes there is an assigned emergency group. The colleagues ought to understand what undertakings and obligations they have during an emergency.

Best practices for dealing with an emergency;

The field of emergency the executives is for the most part considered to have begun with Johnson and Johnson's treatment of a circumstance in 1982, when cyanide-bound Tylenol killed seven individuals in the Chicago region. The organization promptly reviewed all Tylenol containers in the nation and offered free items in carefully designed bundling. Because of the organization's quick and successful reaction, the impact to investors was limited and the brand recuperated and prospered.

Today, basically all large companies, philanthropic offices and public area associations use emergency the board. Creating, rehearsing and refreshing an emergency the board plan is a basic piece of guaranteeing a business can answer unexpected debacles. The idea of the emergency the executives exercises can shift in any case, in view of the association type.

For example, an assembling organization will probably require an emergency the board plan for answering a huge scope modern mishap, like a blast or substance spill, while an insurance agency would be undeniably less inclined to face such dangers.

Obviously, it doesn't accept something as sensational as a modern mishap to require the initiation of an emergency the executives plan. Any occasion that can possibly harm the association's funds or notoriety, might be cause for setting the emergency the executives strategy in motion.

PRE-DRAFT MESSAGES
At last, emergency directors can pre-draft messages that will be utilized during an emergency. All the more precisely, emergency supervisors make layouts for emergency messages. Layouts incorporate proclamations by top administration, news deliveries, and dim sites. Both the Corporate

Administration Committee (2003) and the Business Roundtable (2002) unequivocally suggest the utilization of formats. The formats leave clear places where key data is embedded whenever it is known. Advertising work force can assist with drafting these messages. The legitimate division can then pre-endorse the utilization of the messages. Time is saved during an emergency as unambiguous data is basically embedded and messages sent as well as made accessible on a site.

Chapter 5

BUILDING A CRISIS LEADERSHIP TEAM;

SPOKESPERSON:
A vital part of emergency group preparing is representative preparation. Hierarchical individuals should be ready to converse with the news media during an emergency. significant regard for media relations in an emergency. Media preparing ought to be given before an emergency hits. The Emergency Media Preparing Best Practices in Table 2 were drawn from these three books:

COMMUNICATION CHANNELS;
An association might make a different site for the emergency or assign a part of its ongoing site for the emergency. RESEARCH

finds that having an emergency sites is a best practice for utilizing a Web during an emergency. The site ought to be planned preceding the emergency. This requires the emergency group to expect the sorts of emergencies an association will confront and the kinds of data required for the site. For occasions, any association that makes customer merchandise is probably going to have an item hurt emergency that will require a review.

The worth of an emergency site intended to assist individuals with recognizing in the event that their item is important for the review and how the review will be taken care of. Partners, including the news media, will go to the Web during an emergency. Emergency directors ought to use some type of online reaction or hazard seeming, by all accounts, to be incapable. A genuine model is Taco Ringer's E. coli episode in 2006.

The organization was condemned in the media for being delayed to put emergency related data on its web site. Of course not putting data on the site can be key. An association probably shouldn't pitch the emergency by putting data about it on the site. This expects the emergency is tiny and that partners are probably not going to find out about it from another source. In the present conventional and online media climate, that is an off track on the off chance that not hazardous suspicion.

Stressed that a site is one more method for an association to introduce its side of the story and not utilizing it makes a gamble of losing how the emergency story is told. Intranet locales can likewise be utilized during an emergency. Intranet locales limit access, commonly to representatives just however some will incorporate providers and clients. Intranet locales give direct admittance to explicit partners insofar as those partners approach the Intranet.

Research records the worth of American Carriers' utilization of its Intranet framework as a successful method for speaking with its workers following the 9/11 misfortune. noticed that the correspondence worth of an Intranet site is expanded when utilized related to mass notice frameworks intended to arrive at workers and other key partners. With a mass notice framework, contact data (telephones numbers, email, and so on) are modified in preceding an emergency. Contacts can be any gathering that can be impacted by the emergency including workers, clients, and local area individuals living close to an office.

Emergency administrators can enter short messages into the framework then, at that point, tell the mass warning framework who ought to get which messages and which channel or channels to use for the conveyance. The mass warning framework gives a component to individuals to answer messages too. The reaction include is basic when emergency chiefs need to confirm that the objective has gotten the message. Table 3 sums up the Emergency Correspondence Channel Planning Best Practices.

POST–CRISIS AND RESOLUTION;
After a crisis subsides and business begins to return to normal, the crisis manager should continue to meet with members of the crisis management team, especially those from the legal and finance departments, to evaluate the progression of the recovery efforts. At the same time, the crisis manager will need to provide the latest information to key stakeholders to keep them aware of the current situation.

Following a crisis, it is also important for the crisis management team to revisit the organization's crisis management plan with the goal of evaluating how well the plan worked and what aspects of the plan need to be revised based on what was learned during the crisis.

REPUTATION REPAIR AND BEHAVIORAL INTENTIONS

Various scientists in advertising, correspondence, and showcasing have revealed insight into how to fix the reputational harm an emergency causes for an association. At the focal point of this examination is a rundown of notoriety fix methodologies. Charge Benoit (1995; 1997) has done the most to distinguish the standing fix procedures.

He dissected and blended procedures from a wide range of exploration customs that common a worry for notoriety fix. Table 5 presents the Expert Rundown of Notoriety Fix Systems. The standing fix methodologies differ as far as the amount they oblige casualties of this emergency (those in danger or hurt by the emergency). Oblige implies that the reaction zeros in more on aiding the casualties than on tending to hierarchical worries. The expert rundown organizes the standing fix procedures from the least to the most accommodative standing fix techniques.

Chapter 6

Best practices for all the phase of crisis;

Table 1: Crisis Preparation Best Practices
1. Have a crisis management plan and update it at least annually.
2. Have a designate crisis management team that is properly trained.
3. Conduct exercise at least annually to test the crisis management plan and team.
4. Pre-draft select crisis management messages including content for dark web sites and templates for crisis statements. Have the legal department review and pre-approve these messages.

Table 2: Crisis Media Training Best Practices

1. Avoid the phrase "no comment" because people think it means the organization is guilty and trying to hide something
2. Present information clearly by avoiding jargon or technical terms. Lack of clarity makes people think the organization is purposefully being confusing in order to hide something.

3. Appear pleasant on camera by avoiding nervous habits that people interpret as deception. A spokesperson needs to have strong eye contact, limited disfluencies such as "uhms" or "uhs", and avoid distracting nervous gestures such as fidgeting or pacing. Reports on research that documents how people will be perceived as deceptive if they lack eye contact, have a lot of disfluencies, or display obvious nervous gestures.
4. Brief all potential spokespersons on the latest crisis information and the key message points the organization is trying to convey to stakeholders. Public relations can play a critical role in preparing

spokespersons for handling questions from the news media. The media relations element of public relations is a highly valued skill in crisis management. The public relations personnel can provide training and support because in most cases they are not the spokesperson during the crisis.

Table 3: Crisis Communication Channel Preparation Best Practices
1. Be prepared to use a unique web site or part of your current web site to address crisis concerns.
2. Be prepared to use the Intranet as one of the channels for reaching employees and any other stakeholders than may have access to your Intranet.
3. Be prepared to utilize a mass notification system for reaching employees and other key stakeholders during a crisis

Table 4: Initial Crisis Response Best Practices

1. Be quick and try to have initial response within the first hour.
2. Be accurate by carefully checking all facts.
3. Be consistent by keeping spokespeople informed of crisis events and key message points.
4. Make public safety the number one priority.
5. Use all of the available communication channels including the Internet, Intranet, and mass notification systems.
6. Provide some expression of concern/sympathy for victims
7. Remember to include employees in the initial response.
8. Be ready to provide stress and trauma counseling to victims of the crisis and their families, including employees.

Table 5: Master List of Reputation Repair Strategies

1. Attack the accuser: crisis manager confronts the person or group claiming something is wrong with the organization.
2. Denial: crisis manager asserts that there is no crisis.
3. Scapegoat: crisis manager blames some person or group outside of the organization for the crisis.

4. Excuse: crisis manager minimizes organizational responsibility by denying intent to do harm and/or claiming inability to control the events that triggered the crisis.

Provocation: crisis was a result of response to some one else's actions.

Defeasibility: lack of information about events leading to the crisis situation.

Accidental: lack of control over events leading to the crisis situation.

Good intentions: organization meant to do well

5. Justification: crisis manager minimizes the perceived damage caused by the crisis.
6. Reminder: crisis managers tell stakeholders about the past good works of the organization.
7. Ingratiation: crisis manager praises stakeholders for their actions.
8. Compensation: crisis manager offers money or other gifts to victims.
9. Apology: crisis manager indicates the organization takes full responsibility for the crisis and asks stakeholders for forgiveness.

It should be noted that reputation repair can be used in the crisis response phase, post-crisis phase, or both. Not all crises need reputation repair efforts. Frequently the instructing information and expressions of concern are enough to protect the reputation. When a strong reputation repair effort is required, that effort will carry over into the post-crisis phase. Or, crisis managers may feel more comfortable waiting until the post-crisis phase to address reputation concerns. A list of reputation repair strategies by itself has little utility. Researchers have begun to explore when a specific reputation repair strategy or combination of strategies should be used. These researchers frequently have used attribution theory to develop guidelines for the use of reputation repair strategies. A short explanation of attribution theory is provided along with its relationship to crisis management followed by a summary of lessons learned from this research.

Table 6: Crisis Types by Attribution of Crisis Responsibility
1. Victim Crises: Minimal Crisis Responsibility
2. Natural disasters: acts of nature such as tornadoes or earthquakes.
3. Rumors: false and damaging information being circulated about you organization.

4. Workplace violence: attack by former or current employee on current employees on-site.

5. Product Tampering/Malevolence: external agent causes damage to the organization.

6. Accident Crises: Low Crisis Responsibility

7. Challenges: stakeholder claim that the organization is operating in an inappropriate manner.

8. Technical error accidents: equipment or technology failure that cause an industrial accident.

9. Technical error product harm: equipment or technology failure that cause a product to be defective or potentially harmful.

10. Preventable Crises: Strong Crisis Responsibility

11. Human-error accidents: industrial accident caused by human error.

12. Human-error product harm: product is defective or potentially harmful because of human error.

13. Organizational misdeed: management actions that put stakeholders at risk and/or violate the law.The second step is to review the intensifying factors of crisis history and prior reputation. If an organization has a history of similar crises or has a negative prior reputation, the reputational threat is intensified. A series of experimental studies have documented the intensifying value of crisis history. The same crisis was found to be perceived as having much strong crisis responsibility (a great reputational threat) when the organization had either a previous crisis or the organization was known not to treat stakeholders well/negative prior reputation. Table 7 is a set of crisis communication best practices derived from attribution theory-based research in SCCT.

Table 7: Attribution Theory-based Crisis Communication Best Practices

1. All victims or potential victims should receive instructing information, including recall information. This is one-half of the base response to a crisis.

2. All victims should be provided an expression of sympathy, any information about corrective actions and trauma counseling when needed. This can be called the "care response." This is the second-half of the base response to a crisis.

3. For crises with minimal attributions of crisis responsibility and no intensifying factors, instructing information and care response is sufficient.

4. For crises with minimal attributions of crisis responsibility and an intensifying factor, add excuse and/or justification strategies to the instructing information and care response.

5. For crises with low attributions of crisis responsibility and no intensifying factors,

add excuse and/or justification strategies to the instructing information and care response.

6. For crises with low attributions of crisis responsibility and an intensifying factor, add compensation and/or apology strategies to the instructing information and care response.

7. For crises with strong attributions of crisis responsibility, add compensation and/or apology strategies to the instructing information and care response.

8. The compensation strategy is used anytime victims suffer serious harm.

9. The reminder and ingratiation strategies can be used to supplement any response.

10. Denial and attack the accuser strategies are best used only for rumor and challenge crises.In general, a reputation is how stakeholder perceive an organization. A reputation is widely recognized as a valuable, intangible asset for an organization and is worth protecting. But

the threat posed by a crisis extends to behavioral intentions as well. Increased attributions of organizational responsibility for a crisis result in a greater likelihood of negative word-of-mouth about the organization and reduced purchase intention from the organization. Early research suggests that lessons designed to protect the organization's reputation will help to reduce the likelihood of negative word-of-mouth and the negative effect on purchase intentions as well.

Table 8: Post-Crisis Phase Best Practices
1. Deliver all information promised to stakeholders as soon as that information is known.
2. Keep stakeholders updated on the progression of recovery efforts including any corrective measures being taken and the progress of investigations.

3. Analyze the crisis management effort for lessons and integrate those lessons in to the organization's crisis management system.

Chapter 7

7 STEPS TO CRISIS MANAGEMENT

Every organisation is vulnerable to crises. The days of playing ostrich—burying your head in the sand and hoping the problem goes away–are gone. Crisis management should not merely be reactionary; it should also consist of preventative measures and preparation in anticipation of potential crises. Effective crisis management has the potential to greatly reduce the amount of damage the organization receives as a result of the crisis.

The following steps can help you limit potential damage in a crisis:

1. Anticipate;
The first step is to prepare. Be proactive and arrange an intensive brainstorming session to go through all the potential crises that

could occur at your organisation. The simple rule of thumb is to accept Murphy's Law, "What can go wrong, will go wrong." However, not only are some situations preventable by simply modifying processes, but this assessment process should lead to the creation of a crisis response plan.

2. Create a plan and test it;
The crisis response plan should be tailored for your organisation, and it should include both operational and communications components – in a crisis, what will you do and what will you say? In order to ensure the messages contained in the crisis response plan are delivered effectively and with credibility, it needs to be tested. This is where crisis training and simulations come in, as well as media training for those who could be giving statements and interviews. Most importantly, taking these steps will help ensure you can carry out your response plan in a real-life situation, not just in theory.

3. Identify your crisis communication team; A small team of senior executives should be identified to serve as your organisation's crisis communications team. Ideally, the CEO will lead the team, with the firm's top public relations executive and legal counsel as his or her chief advisers, after that the size if the team depends on the needs of your business.

This team should set the communications process for your business. Avoid getting caught out when a staff member, who does not know the whole story, gives a quote to the media or posts on their personal social media, because they didn't know what to do (or not to do). Make sure a clear process is created and communicated to your staff, channels can include newsletters, employee handbooks and intranet.

4. Establish notification and monitoring systems;

Knowing what's being said about you in traditional and social media, by your employees, customers, and other stakeholders often allows you to catch a negative "trend" that, if unchecked, could turn into a crisis. Likewise, monitoring feedback from stakeholders during a crisis situation allows you to accurately adapt your strategy and tactics. Furthermore, your organisation should have the means to reach the internal and external stakeholders as soon as possible.

5.   Communicate, communicate, communicate;
The first rule of crisis management is to communicate. Early hours are critical and they set the tone for the duration of the crisis. Be as open as possible; tell what you know and when you became aware of it; explain who is involved and what is being done to fix the situation. Be sure to correct misinformation promptly when it emerges. Remaining silent or appearing removed

could enrage the public and other stakeholders.

6. The death of the super injunction;
While crisis experts assert that the legal route is still a valid approach to take, from a reputational point of view, it can sometimes do more harm. Taking legal action can be required at times, but be warned it can cause reputational issues if it looks like you have something to hide or if it looks like you're being greedy. Also, be aware that the legal route takes time. Time is not on your side in a crisis.

7. Post-crisis analysis;
After a crisis, formal analysis of what was done well, what could be done better next time and how to improve various elements of your crisis response plan. This is another must-do activity for any crisis communications team. As the crisis comes under control, a company should examine how effective their plan was during the crisis

and the impact the incident has had on its employees, brand(s) and reputation. If any of those three have taken a hit, a company may need take steps to address them.

Chapter 8

Lessons learned in crisis management;

1. Effect of calamities on investor esteem:

Concentrate on recognized associations that recuperated and, surprisingly, surpassed pre-disaster stock value, (Recoverers), and those that didn't recuperate on stock value, (Non-recoverers). The typical aggregate effect on investor an incentive for the recoverers was 5% in addition to on their unique stock worth. So the net effect on investor esteem by this stage was really sure. The non-recoverers stayed pretty much unaltered between days 5 and 50 after the disaster, however experienced a net negative combined effect of practically 15% on their stock value as long as one year a short time later.

One of the vital finishes of this study is that "Successful administration of the outcomes of calamities would have all the earmarks of being a more huge component than whether disaster protection supports the financial effect of the fiasco".

While there are specialized components to this report it is enthusiastically prescribed to the people who wish to connect with their senior administration in the worth of emergency the executives.

2. Emergency as Any open door:
It is proffers that each emergency is an open door to feature an organization's personality, its obligation to its image guarantee and its institutional qualities. To address such investor influence, the board should move from a mentality that oversees emergency to one that creates emergency

initiative. Research shows that hierarchical contributory elements influence the propensity of chiefs to embrace a compelling "emergency as any open door" mindset.Since pressure is both a precipitator and result of emergency, pioneers who perform well under tension can really direct the association through such emergency.

While the organization's standing with investors, monetary prosperity, and endurance are all in question, likely harm to notoriety can result from the genuine administration of the emergency issue.Additionally, organizations might deteriorate as their gamble the executives bunch recognizes whether an emergency is adequately "measurably huge". Emergency initiative, then again, promptly addresses both the harm and suggestions for the organization's present and future circumstances, as well as any open doors for development.

Need for Crisis Management:
- Emergency The executives readies the people to confront surprising turns of events and unfavorable circumstances in the association with boldness and assurance.
- Representatives change well to the unexpected changes in the association.
- Representatives can comprehend and break down the reasons for emergency and adapt to it in the most ideal manner.

- Emergency The executives assists the supervisors with conceiving methodologies to emerge from questionable circumstances and furthermore settle on the future game-plan.

- Emergency The board assists the chiefs with feeling the early indications of emergency, caution the workers against the aftermaths and play it safe for the equivalent.

Essential Features of Crisis Management
- Emergency The board incorporates exercises and cycles which help the administrators as well as workers to dissect and comprehend occasions which could prompt emergency and vulnerability in the association.
- Emergency The executives empowers the chiefs and workers to answer really to changes in the association culture.

It comprises of successful coordination among the divisions to defeat crisis circumstances.

- Workers at the hour of emergency should discuss successfully with one another and attempt their level best to beat difficult stretches.

Focuses to remember during emergency;

- Try not to frenzy or spread reports around. Show restraint.
- At the hour of emergency the administration ought to be in ordinary touch with the workers, outside clients, partners as well as media.
- Try not to be excessively unbending. One ought to adjust well to changes and new circumstances.

Points to keep in mind during crisis

Don't panic or spread rumours around. Be patient.

At the time of crisis the management should be in regular touch with the employees, external clients, stake holders as well as media.

Avoid being too rigid. One should adapt well to changes and new situations.

CONCLUSION

It is difficult to distill all that is known about crisis management into one, concise entry. I have tried to identify the best practices and lessons created by crisis management researchers and analysts. While crises begin as a negative/threat, effective crisis management can minimize the damage and in some case allow an organization to emerge stronger than before the crisis. However, crises are not the ideal way to improve an organization. But no organization is immune from a crisis so all must do their best to prepare for one.

This entry provides a number of ideas that can be incorporated into an effective crisis management program. At the end of this entry is an annotated bibliography. The annotated bibliography provides short summaries of key writings in crisis management highlighting. Each entry identifies the main topics found in that entry and provides citations to help you locate those sources.

www.ingramcontent.com/pod-product-compliance
Lightning Source LLC
Chambersburg PA
CBHW050309220526
45465CB00005B/1911